CW01646682

The Power of Manifesting
To help you live the life you want

ALLSORTED
for all your gift books and gift stationery

This edition first published in Great Britain in 2024
by Allsorted Ltd., WD19 4BG.

All rights reserved. No part of this work may be reproduced in any form or by any means, electronic or mechanical, including photocopying, recording or by any information storage and retrieval system, without the prior written permission of the publisher.

All information in this publication is for educational and informational purposes. It is not intended as a substitute for professional advice. Should you decide to act upon any information in this publication, you do so at your own risk. While the information in this publication has been verified to the best of our abilities, we cannot guarantee that there are no mistakes or errors.

© Susanna Geoghegan Gift Publishing

Author: Rebecca Dickinson

Illustrator: Jo Parry
Cover and concept design: Jo Parry and Nick Pettit
Contents design: Blackbird Brands

ISBN: 978-1-915902-56-6

Printed in China

10 9 8 7 6 5 4 3 2 1

# Hello dream-seeker

What is it you most desire in life? Whether it's falling in love, landing the perfect job, finding your ideal home, transforming your health and fitness, making a million, launching your own business, travelling the world, or even achieving fame and recognition, we all aspire to something. But how many of us truly believe that our deepest desires can become a reality?

While we all have dreams, often that's all they are: just dreams. "Real life isn't like the movies," you might say. But what if it was? What if there was a way to make the imagined possible? To make the thinkable feasible? Well, by using a range of manifesting techniques, such things can become possible.

This book will help you to understand what manifesting is, and how it works. It will empower you to set intentions, overcome self-limiting beliefs and channel your energy to create the life you've always dreamed of.

"If you see it in your mind, you will hold it in your hand."

*Bob Proctor*

"You are built not to
shrink down to less,
but to blossom into more."

*Oprah Winfrey*

# What is manifesting?

Manifesting can be summed up by the idea that thoughts become things.

At its core, manifesting involves asking the universe to bring your dreams to life. It's a powerful way of attracting the things you want using your thoughts, emotions and actions.

There are many techniques for doing this – visualisations, vision boards, affirmations, practising gratitude, using crystals, meditation, and more – all of which we will explore in this book. But before you can start manifesting, you need to tackle any opposing forces, such as self-doubt, negative thought patterns and limiting beliefs, so we'll address those, too.

However, positive thinking is only part of the story. Manifesting is also about harnessing the laws of attraction. This means aligning your energy with that of the universe by sending out good vibrations. This is at the heart of the positive changes manifesting can bring to our lives – and is where we will start our explorations.

**A gentle disclaimer:** Although positivity is at the heart of manifesting, it's important to recognise and accept all emotions. If you are going through a particularly hard time at the moment, you might want to wait before starting your manifesting journey. Always seek support if you are struggling with your mental or emotional health.

"When you focus on the good, the good gets better."

*Abraham Hicks*

"RULE YOUR MIND OR IT WILL RULE YOU."

Horace

# Understanding the law of attraction

The law of attraction is based on the idea that like attracts like. It is thought that the universe contains energy that causes vibrations, and these vibrations attract anything on the same wavelength. This stems from the theory of relativity which states that atomic energy vibrates at different rates and the particles of an atom are held together by force.

Our thoughts and feelings are also said to contain energy, which is why we sometimes say people give off a 'good vibe'.

According to the law of attraction, positive thoughts and actions attract positive results, and negative thoughts and actions lead to negative outcomes. So, when you send positive energy into the universe – like happiness, gratitude, love, kindness, excitement and enthusiasm – the universe responds on the same energetic wavelength, which can bring about your desired outcome.

To harness the law of attraction you need to:

- focus on your intentions
- take positive action towards your dreams
- believe you will receive.

"Imagination is everything. It is the preview of life's coming attractions."

*Albert Einstein*

"Once you make a decision, the universe conspires to make it happen."

*Albert Einstein*

# Manifesting: Myth versus reality

Manifesting is sometimes regarded as a practice with little or no scientific basis, verging on the mystical. But, in reality, there are no spells or magic wands involved. The bad news is that your dreams are unlikely to come riding in on the back of a unicorn. The good news is that this doesn't make it any less exciting.

At its core, manifesting is a process of personal development where one thing leads to another. It's not a destination, but a journey – with many blessings along the way. And while everyone's journey is unique, the map we use to travel is the same ...

- Release negative emotions and beliefs that may be limiting you from manifesting your desires.
- Cultivate a positive mindset.
- Practise gratitude and kindness to keep raising your positive vibes.

- Set clear intentions and goals to help you progress towards your dreams.

- Focus your energy on the things you want to attract.

- Incorporate techniques such as visualisations, journaling and crystal meditations.

- Maintain an available heart and an open mind.

- Welcome new opportunities and embrace new experiences.

- Celebrate your progress along the way.

- Enjoy the journey and express gratitude unfailingly.

We will explore all these steps in more detail throughout this book.

"It always seems impossible until it's done."

*Nelson Mandela*

“Fully inhale your dream and completely exhale manifestation of it.”

*T.F. Hodge*

# You are worthy

The way you feel about yourself determines your thoughts, feelings and actions – and those thoughts, feelings and actions send out powerful vibrations into the universe. So, before you begin your manifesting journey, spend some time focusing on all your positives and reflecting on the things that make you, you.

Here are some questions to consider. It's a good idea to write down your thoughts in a journal. You might want to ask a friend or family member for some input, too.

- What are you good at?
- What three qualities do you like about yourself?

- What qualities do other people like about you?
- What do you consider to be your best physical features?
- Name three compliments you've received.
- What three things are you most proud of in your life?

You might find singing your own praises uncomfortable at first, but this isn't a bragging exercise; think of it as acknowledging your self-worth. Actively focusing on your unique and special qualities builds confidence and self-esteem, which helps you to believe you are worthy of attracting and receiving blessings.

“Just one small positive thought in the morning can change your whole day.”

*Dalai Lama*

"Don't you ever let a soul in the world tell you that you can't be exactly who you are."

*Lady Gaga*

# Tame your inner critic

We are all guilty of self-criticism from time to time. However, since you can only manifest from a place of positivity, that internal critical voice is one of the main barriers to realising your dreams.

Here are some tactics to help get your inner saboteur under control.

- **Notice when a negative thought pops into your head:** This can be helpful in trying to understand when, and why, such thoughts occur.
- **Examine the evidence:** Would your negative thought stand up in court? If not, you can assume it's untrue and unhelpful.

- **What would you say to a friend?** Often, it's easier to be more compassionate towards others than it is to ourselves.
- **Flip your thought around:** Consider what would happen if the opposite were true. Thinking in this way can help shift your awareness from the negative to the positive.
- **Keep a sense of perspective:** Ask yourself: How will I feel about this tomorrow, or next week, or next month, or even next year?

Silencing your inner critic doesn't happen overnight, but with practice you can replace it with an inner cheerleader.

"WE ARE ALL OF US STARS, AND WE DESERVE TO TWINKLE."

Marilyn Monroe

"You are enough

just as you are."

*Meghan Markle*

# Give yourself some love

When you love someone, you want the best for them – so it's important to apply the same rule to yourself. Practising self-care isn't selfish; it's vital for your wellbeing. It also sends a message to your inner self – and the universe – that you are worthy of blessings. However busy you are, try to make time for the things that help you feel good.

- **Treat yourself:** We all know the importance of healthy eating, but that doesn't mean you can't indulge now and then. So, make space in your week for your favourite meal, have some chocolate or let someone else do the cooking for a change.

- **Pamper yourself:** Paint your nails, do a face mask, exfoliate, or book a massage or a facial at the end of a long week.

- **Unwind:** Whether it's meditating, having a power nap or just making time for a coffee break, taking a conscious pause provides a vital antidote to the stresses of modern life and helps avoid burnout.

- **Let your hair down:** Dance, be silly, play a game, hang out with friends, watch a comedy – whatever makes you happy. Having fun makes us feel energised and boosts positive emotions.

"If you get tired, learn to rest, not to quit."

*Banksy*

"You are the sum total of everything you've ever seen, heard, eaten, smelled, been told, forgot."

*Maya Angelou*

# Let it go

This exercise is designed to help you release the blockages that may be holding you back. Giving shelter to negative feelings, such as anger, sadness, hurt and resentment, can prevent you from living the life you want. Releasing these feelings can be painful and take time, but will result in a sense of inner peace and freedom, creating space for new energy to flow.

**Step 1: Ask yourself questions**

- What grudges am I holding on to?
- Am I harbouring ill-feelings towards anyone in my life, or anyone from my past?
- What negative memories or emotions are standing in the way of my future?
- What do I need to let go of?

### Step 2: Say goodbye

- Write down your answers on as many sheets of paper as you need. Then, tear the paper into shreds.
- Now, find somewhere safe to set fire to your shredded paper.
- Watch as flames engulf your words. Imagine all the negative emotions inside you turning to ash as you say to yourself, "I let go of everything that doesn't serve me."

> **A note of caution:** This exercise can stir painful emotions. Always seek professional help if you need support to work through any of the issues that arise.

"Don't let the sadness from the past and the fear of the future ruin the happiness of the present."

*Wiz Khalifa*

"And the day came when
the risk to remain tight
in a bud was more painful
than the risk it took
to blossom."

*Elizabeth Appell*

# Ready, set, manifest

Now that you have done some of the soul work – a kind of inner MOT, if you like – it's time to get on the road. There are three basic elements of manifesting: intention, attention and permission.

- **1. Set your intentions:** This is all about identifying your dreams. Be bold and ask yourself what it is that your heart truly desires. Focus on one area of your life that you would like to transform, then map out the details.

- **2. Direct your attention:** This involves focusing your energy and awareness on the thing you'd like to manifest using techniques that feel right for you, such as meditation, visualisation, writing or using crystals. You will find exercises for all these throughout this book.

- **3. Give yourself permission:** For the final piece of the manifesting jigsaw, you need to allow yourself to receive the fruits of your energy. This might sound silly, but in order to receive good things, you need to believe that you deserve them. This could involve doing some inner work to embrace your self-worth and overcome negativity, as well as practising self-care.

**Try:** Change the screensaver on your phone to an image that represents your manifestation – as a way of embedding it in your subconscious.

“Wherever you go,
go with all your heart.”

*Confucius*

“If you can dream it,
you can do it.”

*Walt Disney*

# Follow your heart

It can be easy to succumb to the pressure of 'should' and 'ought', and to bow to other people's expectations of how we should live. However, when our actions conflict with our values, this can leave us feeling uncomfortable and unfulfilled.

For manifesting to be successful, it must sit comfortably with your own principles and with the things that matter to you, personally. You can only bring into your life the things that you choose for yourself with your own free will. The key is simply this: follow your heart.

Take some uninterrupted time to get in touch with your heart and acknowledge your true desires. Take a pen and notebook and write down the first things that come to mind when you think about the following questions.

- When do you feel at your happiest?
- When do you feel most alive?
- What are your wildest dreams?
- What secret ambitions do you hold?
- What did you daydream about as a child?
- If you could do anything in life, what would it be?
- If you could go anywhere, where would you go?

"The only thing that will make you happy is being happy with who you are, and not who people think you are."

*Goldie Hawn*

"LIFE ISN'T ABOUT FINDING YOURSELF. LIFE IS ABOUT CREATING YOURSELF."

George Bernard Shaw

# Try an intention-setting exercise

Once you have spent some time reflecting on the desires of your heart, use this exercise to set your intentions.

- **Write it down:** Take a sheet of paper, or a journal, and tell the universe what it is you desire.
- **Focus on the details:** For example, if you want a new job, don't just write 'new job', write down everything about it – as if you already had it: your salary, your location, your role and responsibilities. If you want to attract a partner, note down everything about them: their physical features, age and background. Doing this provides clarity on what your desire looks like in real life. It also helps you connect with the emotions of living out your dream.

- **Check in with your intentions daily:** It's good practice to do this in the same place, at the same time, every day. Try to imagine you have already reached your goal, then dwell on those emotions. Feeling the happiness or abundance that accompanies your goal, as if you have already achieved it, helps supercharge the manifestation process. And finally: be patient.

“A seed hidden in the heart of an apple is an orchard invisible.”

*Welsh proverb*

"Those who don't believe in magic will never find it."

*Arianna Huffington*

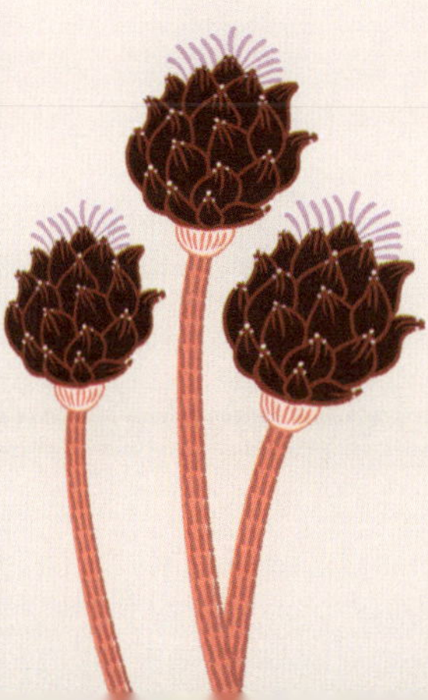

# Create a vision board

A vision board is a collection, or collage, of images that represents your dreams and aspirations. This is a powerful tool for manifesting since it is a physical reminder of your dreams. By looking at your vision board every day, you will become more motivated to reach your goals.

Here are some tips to help you create your own vision board.

- Start by choosing a theme. It could be an area of your life you'd like to manifest, such as your career, relationships or health.
- You will need some kind of board – a corkboard is great, or you could use a magnetic board, a whiteboard or, alternatively, create a digital board if you prefer.

- Gather some images that represent your vision. These could include photographs, magazine cuttings, pieces of fabric or even objects from nature, such as feathers and leaves. You could add some quotes, too.

- Arrange your images on your board until you're happy with the way it looks. Feel free to embellish it with doodles, stickers or other craft materials.

- Hang your vision board somewhere prominent and allow it to fill you with joy and excitement every time you look at it.

“Just be yourself,

there is no one better.”

*Louisa May Alcott*

"Without dreams and goals there is no living, only merely existing, and that is not why we are here."

*Paulo Coelho*

# Create a manifesting space

You've heard of she-sheds and man-caves. Well, a manifesting space is like a private sanctuary, just for manifesting. It doesn't have to be a whole room; a quiet corner or a little spot outdoors is perfect, just so long as it's somewhere you feel happy, calm and inspired.

Here are some tips to help you create your own, personal manifesting space.

- **Get rid of clutter:** Old, unwanted items don't just look messy, they can cause you to remain stuck in the past. A clear space allows energy to flow freely.

- **Make it comfortable:** Your space needs to be inviting, so think about lighting, soft furnishings and seating. For example, consider a salt lamp, fairy lights or candles; cushions and throws; a beanbag or other comfortable place to sit.

- **Focus on the sacred:** Your manifesting space is somewhere you can connect with the universe, so try to include items that amplify your energy, such as incense, crystals, mandalas, dreamcatchers or objects from nature. You might like to create a simple altar or shrine.

- **Make it personal:** Include objects that reflect your desires, such as photographs, inspiring prints, a vision board or other meaningful items. If you are manifesting wealth, for example, you might want to add some carefully placed coins.

"The secret of change is to focus all of your energy not on fighting the old, but on building the new."

*Dan Millman*

“The future belongs to those who believe in the beauty of their dreams.”

*Eleanor Roosevelt*

# The power of affirmations

Affirmations are short, positive statements that can be used as a powerful tool for overcoming negative thoughts and bringing positive changes into your life. They also help you to remain focused.

The key is to repeat your affirmations regularly. For maximum impact, try reciting them as soon as you wake up in the morning and just before you go to sleep at night. This is when your brain produces alpha waves, so your subconscious is at its most receptive. The more you repeat your affirmations, the more your brain perceives them as a reality.

Try writing your affirmations on postcards and sticking them in a prominent position, like the bathroom mirror or the fridge. It's important to choose affirmations that mean something to you, personally. Here are some examples to get you started.

- I surrender to the universe.
- I am attracting the things I want into my life.
- Everything I desire is within my power.
- I already have so much to be thankful for.
- Good things are happening to me all the time.
- Everything I need is already within me.
- Positive energy flows through me.

Saying your affirmations out loud reinforces your intentions and reminds you of your worth.

"What you think, you become.
What you feel, you attract.
What you imagine, you create."

*Unknown*

"It's easy to hear the voices of others and often very difficult to hear your own. Every person you meet is going to want something different from you. The question is: what do you want for yourself?"

*Beyoncé Knowles*

# Be the energy you want to attract

Manifesting involves channelling your thoughts and energy to align with your desires. So, what you think about, you will bring into your life. This means that by focusing on positive thoughts and actions, you will attract more positive things into your life.

However, the reverse is also true. Remember: like attracts like. So, if you focus on what you don't have, rather than what you do have, you will only attract more of the thing you don't have. If you focus on problems, you will attract more problems.

For example, if you want to manifest wealth but keep telling yourself, "I don't have enough money," your focus remains on feeling poor, and you will only manifest a continued lack of money, not the financial freedom you desire.

To overcome this, it is essential to frame your attention positively by focusing on abundance. So, in the case of money, you might shift your internal dialogue to saying, "I'm so grateful that I have enough money to buy delicious food and to keep myself warm."

Reframing your narrative raises your energy levels and the universe will respond accordingly, allowing your dreams to unfold.

"THE MOST COMMON WAY PEOPLE GIVE UP THEIR POWER IS BY THINKING THEY DON'T HAVE ANY."

Alice Walker

"I have learned over the years that when one's mind is made up, this diminishes fear; knowing what must be done does away with fear."

*Rosa Parks*

# Try a visualisation exercise

Have you ever been so lost in a daydream that you felt like you'd been transported to another time or place? The aim of visualisation is to trick your mind into believing the daydream is reality. This elevates your energy, triggering the law of attraction, which is the key to manifesting your desires.

Choose a dream you would like to visualise and then follow these steps.

- Find a quiet spot, get into a comfortable position and close your eyes. Take three slow, deep breaths, then breathe normally.
- Set your intention by stating either aloud or in your head, "I manifest ..."

- Start by imagining that you are in the cinema, watching yourself on screen. Your dream life is playing out and you are the star. Notice what you look like and your surroundings. What are you are doing? Who you are with?

- Next, imagine stepping into the screen – it's no longer a movie, but real life. You are living your dream. Allow yourself to become fully immersed in the experience, using your senses to take in the colours, smells and sounds. Spend some time revelling in your emotions.

- Say to yourself, "I am living the life I desire."

"As you think,
you travel,
and as you love,
you attract."

*James Lane Allen*

"For there is nothing either good or bad, but thinking makes it so."

*William Shakespeare*

# Get the feels

An important aspect of manifesting is allowing your mind to experience the emotions associated with your desires – before you've actually achieved them.

Tapping into the joy and excitement reinforces your desires in your subconscious mind while boosting your positive energy. Try to imagine this positive energy as vibrations. The stronger your positive energy, the stronger the vibrations you send out into the universe. In this way, you are brought closer to whatever it is you want to manifest.

Positive affirmations and visualisations are both great ways of connecting to the feeling of achieving your desires. Here are some more things to try.

- **Reflect on your goals before going to sleep:** Making your desires the last thing you think about at night helps them slide into your subconscious.

- **Surround yourself with people who lift you up:** Positive emotions are contagious!

- **Strike a power pose and stand like a superhero:** head held high, chest out, hands on hips. It's not as silly as it sounds: your body language really can influence the way you feel.

- **Fake it till you make it:** This doesn't mean lying, but rather acting as if you are the person you want to become. Studies show that changing your behaviour can change the way you feel.

"Your mind is a garden.
Your thoughts are the seeds.
You can grow flowers
or you can grow weeds."

*Unknown*

“Whatever you believe with feeling becomes your reality.”

*Brian Tracy*

# Try a goal-setting exercise

Once you've set your intentions and placed your desires in the palm of the universe, it's time to figure out your next move. Whatever it is you want to manifest, try using the SMART goals model to help you get there.

**SMART** goals will help you to clarify your ideas, concentrate your efforts and make the best use of the resources and time that you have available to succeed in your goals.

**SMART** stands for:

**Specific:**
For example, don't just say you want a new job – have a specific job in mind. Clear goals lead to clear results, so be as unambiguous as possible.

**Measurable:**
It's a good idea to break down big goals into smaller ones. This enables you to identify tangible checkpoints and tick them off one by one.

**Achievable:**

It's great to challenge yourself, but your goals need to be within your capabilities. For example, you're unlikely to become a Premier League footballer if you've never kicked a ball before, but you could start by joining a local club.

**Realistic:**

SMART goals also need to be manageable. For example, if you want to run a marathon, have you got enough time to train? Are you medically fit enough?

**Time-bound:**

Set yourself a schedule to help keep you focused and a deadline to help you reach the end result.

“Manifestation without action is only a wish.”

*Nanette Mathews*

“I am realistic

– I expect miracles.”

*Wayne W. Dyer*

# Get in the zone

Manifesting is an amazing way to bring change into your life. By using positive thoughts to trigger the law of attraction, you will become a magnet for new and exciting opportunities.

However, you can't just sit back and wait for the universe to deliver. If you want results, you need to get out there. You need to step outside your comfort zone and into the energy zone. Here are some ways to keep moving forwards.

- **Take risks:** It can be tempting to settle for an easy life, but facing up to challenges is the only way to step into your full potential and manifest your desires.

- **Learn new skills:** Broadening your skill set and deepening your knowledge boosts your confidence and self-esteem – and it proves you are capable of growing.

- **Celebrate success:** Accept the compliments, acknowledge the feedback, own your good work! Taking pride in how far you have come propels you to go further.

- **Look after your health and wellbeing:** You won't reach your goals if you're running on empty, so don't neglect your physical needs. These include eating well, getting enough sleep, exercising and making time for relaxation.

"When we believe that life is a gift, life rewards us with miracles."

*Milan Ljubincic*

"I DWELL IN POSSIBILITY."

Emily Dickinson

# Reset your mindset

Manifesting and positivity are like two sides of the same coin. With positive intentions, positive actions and positive thoughts you can manifest your deepest desires. First, though, you need to work on your mindset. There are two types of mindset.

- **People with a growth mindset** believe their skills and abilities can be developed over time. This motivates them to keep working towards their goals.
- **People with a fixed mindset** believe their skills and abilities are fixed. This means they are more likely to give up when they find something difficult.

Having a growth mindset is essential for manifesting because it's linked to confidence, resilience and positivity. The good news is that science shows us the brain is malleable, which means we can all develop a growth mindset. Here are some tips.

- Start with small, achievable goals to build your confidence.
- Believe in your potential for growth and change.
- Acknowledge that every challenge is an opportunity to learn and improve.
- Celebrate the learning process, not just the results.
- Use setbacks as a chance to practise or try a different approach.
- When things go wrong, focus on how you can improve instead of feeling discouraged.

"Don't let anyone tell you what you can or cannot do, or cannot achieve. Do not allow it."

*Emma Watson*

"Progress is not inevitable.
It's up to us to create it."

*Michael Bloomberg*

# How to keep the toxic out of positivity

The expression 'good vibes only' is one that's often associated with manifesting. The practice of manifestation is founded on the idea that you can control your life by controlling your thoughts: positive thoughts lead to positive outcomes. Realising this can be amazingly empowering and rewarding; it can even be life-changing. But ...

Problems can arise when we fail to acknowledge our struggles, or when we do not allow ourselves to accept any kind of negative emotions. The truth is, no one feels 100% positive, 100% of the time. Placing yourself under this kind of pressure by taking positivity to an extreme simply isn't healthy – subjecting yourself to toxic positivity can actually be harmful. Real life can be messy and painful, complicated and confusing – and that's completely normal.

It's vital to acknowledge and work through all your emotions, including the negative, sad and difficult ones. Lean on the people around you and seek professional help if you need extra support.

Accepting the good as well as the bad might not be much fun at the time, but dealing with difficult situations and emotions allows you to heal and grow as a person. And this, in the long run, will enable you to manifest your dream life.

“You may not control all the events that happen to you, but you can decide not to be reduced by them.”

*Maya Angelou*

"The unexamined life is not worth living."

*Socrates*

# The power of meditation

Meditation is a powerful way to clear your mind, leading to a sense of inner peace. Scientific research shows that regularly practising meditation can have a profound effect on your health and wellbeing. It's even been shown to bring about physical changes in the brain, increasing the regions associated with learning, memory and controlling emotions, and decreasing the amygdala – the part of the brain involved in stress.

When you meditate, you allow yourself to 'just be'. This awakens the mind to a deeper level of consciousness, enabling you to distance yourself from negative or distracting thoughts. With practice, you will find this helps you to feel more energised, focused and alert, and more in tune with yourself and the universe. This creates the perfect foundation from which to manifest.

There are many ways to meditate. If you haven't tried it before, the easiest way to start is to choose a word, or mantra, such as 'peace' or 'om' and repeat it inside your head for a few minutes. Try doing this in a quiet space at a regular time each day – and notice the difference it makes to the way you feel.

"All that we are is
the result of what
we have thought."

*Ralph Waldo Emerson*

"WE DON'T SEE THINGS AS THEY ARE, WE SEE THEM AS WE ARE."

Anaïs Nin

# Choose gratitude

Developing an attitude of gratitude has been scientifically proven to enhance your health and wellbeing. It's also the starting point from which to successfully manifest.

Expressing gratitude enables you to appreciate all the good things in your life. Crucially, it also draws you away from focusing on what you don't have. This is vital to manifesting, since you can't manifest from a sense of lack.

What's more, when you are grateful you send positive vibrations into the universe, which enables you to attract more good things. It's a win–win situation.

Take some time to reflect on the things you are grateful for. Here are a few examples to start you off.

- **Your body:** For all the unseen miracles that take place in your cells every second of every day, helping to keep you alive.
- **Food:** For providing nourishment and pleasure.
- **Friends and family:** For the laughs, the hugs, the support and the sense of belonging.
- **Nature:** For the artistry of a sunset, the beauty of a flower, the majesty of mountains and the wonder of the night sky.
- **Transport:** For the chance to travel both near and far, to be reunited, to come home, and to explore.

"Turn your face toward
the sun and the shadows
will fall behind you."

*Māori proverb*

"Count your age by friends, not years. Count your life by smiles, not tears."

*John Lennon*

# Choose kindness

Like gratitude, kindness is another wonderful way to increase positive emotions. And since like attracts like, you will attract more kindness and generosity into your own life, too.

When you are kind towards someone, you don't just enhance their life, you enrich your own life as well. Studies show that when we carry out acts of kindness, this causes the brain to release endorphins, triggering a surge in happiness and positivity – also known as the 'helper's high'.

Being kind towards others also tells the universe that you are ready to receive blessings into your own life. It's like giving your manifesting journey the green light.

Here are just a few ways to make kindness a part of your life.

- Volunteering
- Donating time or money to charity
- Being inclusive
- Caring for others and showing compassion
- Being considerate, for example, giving up your seat on a bus or letting someone go in front of you in a queue
- Listening attentively
- Offering practical support, such as a lift or a helping hand
- Sharing your skills and expertise

**Tip:** Keeping a kindness and gratitude journal is a great way to make these qualities part of your mindset.

"Let no one ever come
to you without leaving
better and happier."

*Mother Teresa*

"How you love yourself
is how you teach others
to love you."

*Rupi Kaur*

# Try an anchoring technique

Anchoring is a means of connecting a positive memory to a physical stimulus. The happy memory allows you to reconnect to the energy of the past, while the anchor brings it to the present – so it's a great way to support your manifesting.

Follow these steps to begin making these stimulus–response connections.

- Think of a time when you felt amazing – for example, a wonderful holiday, an incredible meal, or perhaps an electrifying date.

- Spend a few moments basking in the memory. Make the image really bold, vibrant and clear, allowing yourself to relive the emotions as if you are actually there.

- Now choose an anchor that works for you – for example, pressing your thumb and forefinger together, touching a specific object (such as a keyring or a piece of jewellery), inhaling a particular scent, or listening to a certain song.
- As you consciously relive your positive experience, activate your chosen stimulus – for example, by squeezing your thumb and forefinger together.
- Use your anchor whenever you need to revisit your memory and experience the emotions it evokes. Your anchor is now an instant shortcut to positivity and confidence.

"Ask for what you want
and be prepared to get it."

*Maya Angelou*

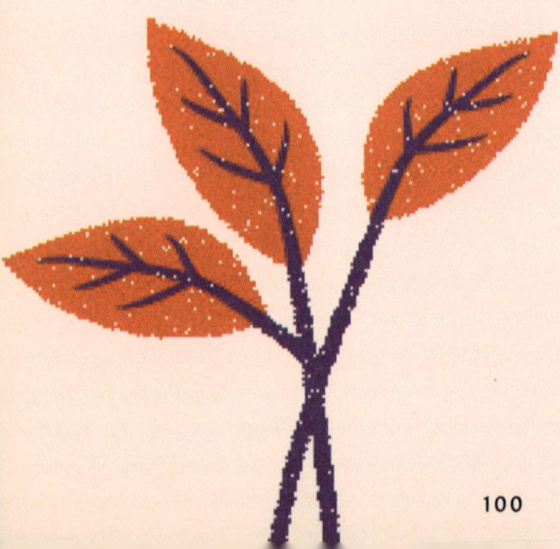

“Know your magic, trust your magic, use your magic and know that you are a manifestation of life’s magic.”

*Rasheed Ogunlaru*

# The power of crystals

Humans have been captivated by crystals since time immemorial. The word 'crystal' comes from the Greek word krystallos, meaning both 'ice' and 'rock crystal' as the ancient Greeks believed clear quartz was ice frozen so hard it couldn't melt.

In fact, these rare, beautiful and mysterious minerals are formed underground, reminding us of our connection to the Earth. They are characterised by their repeating geometric patterns – a reflection of the highly organised internal layout of atoms. It's this incredible, intricate arrangement that determines the crystal's properties and uses, including shape, colour and size.

Crystals have been associated with spirituality since ancient times, but they are just as relevant today and are the perfect companion for manifesting. Despite their outer stillness, crystals are believed to be a powerful source of energy, composed of a mass of tiny, vibrating atomic particles. For this reason, they are often used in healing and to promote positivity and to cleanse negative energy.

Always buy crystals that have been sourced without harm to people or the planet. An ethical retailer should be able to provide information about the origin of their gemstones and how they were mined. If they can't give you a clear answer, look elsewhere. Beware too, of crystals that are cheaply priced as this may indicate that the miners haven't been paid fairly.

"THE CRYSTAL IS A UNIVERSAL SYMBOL OF BALANCE, HARMONY, AND UNITY."

Masaru Emoto

"Every crystal holds a little bit of magic."

*Unknown*

# Some crystals to consider

There are hundreds of different crystals, all with individual properties and energies. Different crystals can be used to help you manifest specific areas of your life.

## Crystals for manifesting health

- **Clear quartz:** This is considered to be a master healer, used to dispel negative energy.
- **Jasper:** Jasper is a nurturing crystal, perfect for times of stress.
- **Amethyst:** This crystal is widely used for healing and purifying, and for bringing peace and mental clarity.
- **Malachite:** Malachite is believed to promote sleep.
- **Obsidian:** Obsidian is said to help process emotions and to help with letting go.
- **Bloodstone:** This stone is believed to improve circulation.

### Crystals for manifesting wealth

- **Turquoise:** Turquoise is associated with soothing the emotions and attracting good luck.
- **Yellow sapphire:** This stone is sometimes known as the 'stone of prosperity'.
- **Jade:** Jade is known for prosperity and luck.
- **Carnelian:** A stone associated with happiness and attracting abundance.

### Crystals for manifesting love

- **Rose quartz:** Known as the 'heart stone' or 'stone of love', it is used for emotional healing and romance.
- **Ruby:** Thought to promote sexuality and sensuality.
- **Moonstone:** It is believed that moonstone can aid inner strength and growth.

"Remember ... hope is a good thing, maybe the best of things, and no good thing ever dies."

*Stephen King*

"I carry a lot of rose quartz, which attracts the male. Maybe I need to calm it down with amethyst."

*Katy Perry*

# Choosing and caring for your crystals

Different crystals have different vibrational energies, so it's important to choose one that's right for you. Here are some tips to help.

Decide what you'd like your crystal to help with – for example, a sense of peace, or increased confidence. Spend some time researching which crystals match your needs.

When purchasing a crystal, let your intuition lead the way. You might want to close your eyes and take a few deep breaths. When you open your eyes, you may find you're drawn to one particular crystal. If you're still not sure, you could try saying: "Please may I work with you?" If you get a sense of peace, the answer is 'yes'.

It's also absolutely fine to choose a crystal that appeals to you visually, since you're more likely to connect with a crystal that you like the look of.

## Cleansing your crystals

Before manifesting with your crystals, it's important to cleanse them of any previous negative energy they may have absorbed. One method is to hold your crystals under running water then leave them in direct sunlight. Or, if there's a full moon, leave them outside to recharge in moonlight.

Another way of cleansing crystals is to bury them in the earth for 24 hours; when you dig them up the following day, they'll have been cleansed and recharged. Just make sure you know exactly where you've buried your crystals – and that nothing else is likely to dig them up first!

"In a crystal, we have clear evidence of the existence of a formative life principle, and though we cannot understand the life of a crystal, it is nonetheless a living being."

*Nikola Tesla*

"You know the world is a magical place when Mother Nature grows her own jewellery."

*Unknown*

# Manifesting with crystals

By tapping into the energetic power of crystals, you can unblock, focus and direct your energy to manifest your dreams. First, cleanse your crystal, and then follow these steps.

- Hold your crystal in your dominant hand and empty your mind of distractions and unwanted thoughts.

- Focus on the crystal in your palm and set your intentions. Remember to frame your desires positively. For example, if you want to manifest money you might say, "I am open to greater prosperity."

- Repeat your intention out loud until you feel aligned. Some people feel a warm or tingling sensation at this point.

- To get the most out of your crystal, keep it near you. For example, place it under your pillow, on your desk, or carefully store it in a pocket or bag. Alternatively, you might want to wear it as a piece of jewellery. Staying close to your crystal's vibrations can raise your own energy.

- You can also incorporate your crystal into techniques like yoga and meditation; just keep it nearby when you're engaged in these practices.

- Enjoy being in your crystal's presence.

"Keep calm and hold a crystal."

*Unknown*

"Crystals are nature's artwork."

*Unknown*

# Try a crystal meditation exercise

Meditation can transport you to a place of inner peace and clarity – so incorporating crystals into your practice can be a powerful way to enhance this and support your manifesting journey.

- Sit in a comfortable, upright position; hold your crystal in one hand, palms facing upwards.
- Close your eyes and take a few slow, deep breaths.
- Bring your awareness to your crystal and visualise it growing larger and larger until it's sitting in front of you.
- Next, imagine dazzling rays of light radiating from your crystal. Focus on the colours and the brightness.
- Visualise these rays enveloping you with warmth and protection.

- As the glow surrounds you, feel the energy of your crystal mingling with that of your own, amplifying your vibrations.

- As your energies align, visualise whatever it is you hope to manifest. Picture it wrapped in clear, bright light. Inhale this light, allowing it to fill you with peace and clarity.

- Remain in this beautiful moment for as long as you desire. Then, when you are ready, slowly return your awareness to your surroundings and open your eyes.

- At the end of your meditation, take a moment to express gratitude towards your crystal.

“Realize deeply that the present moment is all you ever have.”

*Eckhart Tolle*

"THE ONLY WAY TO LIVE IS BY ACCEPTING EACH MINUTE AS AN UNREPEATABLE MIRACLE."

Tara Brach

# Try journaling

Writing down your thoughts and desires increases your self-awareness and is an effective way to declutter your mind. It's also a powerful tool for manifesting, helping you to make sense of your goals and focus on achieving them.

There are no rules when it comes to journaling; it's your story to write your way – spelling mistakes and all! The key is to write as if no one is reading (unless you allow them to). If you're not sure what to include in your journal, here are some ideas.

- **Your vision for the future:** Define what you would like to achieve and receive – and how you will go about making it happen. Keep coming back to this page to keep your goals alive in your mind.

- **Positive affirmations:** Including positive affirmations in your journal helps you to reprogramme your subconscious. For example:

  I am worthy.
  I am strong.

- **A gratitude list:** You can never have too much gratitude. Curating a list of the things you are thankful for is a great way to feed your positivity.

- **Some fun:** There's no need to limit your journal to words alone; stickers, doodles, pictures and photographs can all add colour and excitement to your story!

**Tip:** Aim to be consistent by setting aside a regular time of the day for journaling.

“The bad news is time flies.
The good news is you’re
the pilot.”

*Michael Altshuler*

"It's no good being too easily swayed by people's opinions. You have to believe in yourself."

*Donatella Versace*

## Try a scripting technique

This exercise is like writing a journal entry, only for a day you haven't yet lived – a day in the future. It's a fun way of creating a detailed picture of something you want to manifest.

The important thing is to write in the present tense, as if you have already achieved your desire. This aligns your subconscious with your dream life, tricking your mind into thinking it's a reality.

- Choose a desire you would like to manifest and pick a day in the future.
- Starting with the words 'I am ...', describe your waking moments. Include plenty of detail. What do you have

for breakfast? What colour is your kitchen? How does the sun stream through the blinds? What are you wearing?

- Starting with the words 'I go ...', write about your day as it unfolds. Where do you go? Who do you meet? What conversations do you have?

- Starting with the words 'I'm so excited because ...', describe your emotions as you go about your day. Cultivate these feelings as you write.

- Carry on writing – describing your day, hour by hour – until you finally go to bed, happy and fulfilled.

"You define your own life. Don't let other people write your script."

*Oprah Winfrey*

"Optimism is the faith that leads to achievement. Nothing can be done without hope and confidence."

*Helen Keller*

# The 369 method

One of the ingredients for successful manifestation is repetition. This technique is very simple and easily manageable. It is attributed to the inventor Nikola Tesla, who believed that the numbers three, six and nine were powerful for unlocking the laws of the universe.

All you need to do is grab your journal (writing by hand is better than using a phone or laptop) and note down your manifestation:

- three times when you wake up
- six times at midday
- nine times before you go to sleep.

As you write, remember to:

- be thankful – begin with gratitude for what you already have
- be specific – make sure your manifestation is very clear and focused
- write as if it's already happened.

**Tip:** If you don't have time for the 369 technique, try adapting it to suit your lifestyle. For example, you could try a 333, or even a 33, method. The important thing is consistency. This helps focus the mind, which brings you closer to your goals.

"If you want to find the secrets of the universe, think in terms of energy, frequency and vibration."

*Nikola Tesla*

You are what you think about all day long."

Dr Robert Schuller

# Get to know your chakras

Your chakras are energy centres within your body that correspond to different feelings and bodily systems.

Many cultures believe that the chakras play a vital role in health and wellbeing, and that when your chakras are aligned, the mind, body and spirit can exist in harmony. This, in turn, enhances your ability to manifest.

There are thought to be seven major chakras in the body, running from the base of your spine to the top of your head.

- **Root chakra:** This is situated at the base of the spine; it helps us feel confident and grounded.
- **Sacral chakra:** This sits just below the belly button and is related to emotions, creativity and sexuality.

- **Solar plexus chakra:** Located around the abdomen, this is linked to self-esteem.
- **Heart chakra:** As the name suggests, this chakra governs love and compassion.
- **Throat chakra:** Located around the voice, this enables us to communicate.
- **Third-eye chakra:** Positioned between the eyes, this chakra is responsible for intuition.
- **Crown chakra:** The crown chakra– located at the crown of the head – provides our spiritual connection with the universe.

"When the crown chakra opens, the 1000 petals of the perfect bliss arises. You will find no mud but nutrients."

*Amit Ray*

"There is deep wisdom within our very flesh, if we can only come to our senses and feel it."

*Elizabeth Behnke*

# Balancing your chakras

When your chakras are open, energy flows through them freely. But when one or more of your chakras are blocked, your mind, body and spirit suffer. This can result in physical illness and emotional unrest. It can also inhibit the ability to manifest.

Rebalancing your chakras won't just make you feel better, it will unblock your energetic potential to manifest, too. There are many ways to unblock your chakras, including crystal healing and reiki. Here are some things you can try at home.

- **Connect with nature:** Spending time outdoors is a wonderful way to ground yourself and absorb the healing energy of Mother Earth. Try walking barefoot for an extra boost.

- **Yoga:** The mindful movements of yoga help you to feel connected to your breath and the ground, supporting chakra health.

- **Meditation:** Clearing space in your mind creates space for energy to flow.

- **Breathing exercises:** Breathing techniques promote relaxation and can help release the emotions that hold us back.

- **Essential oils:** Inhaling the fragrances of different oils, for example in a bath or a diffuser, is another lovely way to soothe your emotions and rebalance your chakras.

"The body never lies."

*Martha Graham*

"Disease is often an accumulation of dammed-up energy. When we learn how energy moves through the chakras, we can begin to allow it to flow freely through our bodies, creating greater health."

*Caroline Shola Arewa*

# Recharge

Keeping your energy levels elevated is crucial for manifesting. But it's not all chakras and crystals. It's important to look after your more elementary needs, too. This includes getting enough sleep. You can't manifest if you're sleep-deprived, so here are some tips to help you get a better night.

- **Stick to a regular routine:** It may sound dull, but going to bed and getting up at the same time every day really is the key to better sleep.

- **Get an earlier night:** Start by bringing your bedtime forwards by 15 minutes each day until getting up in the morning is no longer a chore.

- **Shun lie-ins:** Yes, the duvet is warm and the snooze button is calling – but don't, whatever you do, give in.

- **Get outside:** Natural morning light triggers your body to stop producing melatonin, the chemical that makes you sleepy. This has a knock-on effect in the evening, helping to regulate your circadian rhythm.

- **Add some activity:** Fitting some exercise into your day makes it more likely you'll sleep well at night. However, avoid exercising within three hours of going to bed as this can have the opposite effect!

"For you to sleep well at night, the aesthetic, the quality, has to be carried all the way through."

*Steve Jobs*

"The best bridge between despair and hope is a good night's sleep."

*E. Joseph Cossman*

# Tune in to nature

One of the most powerful ways to connect with the universe is to spend time in nature. Stepping away from our concrete, technological environments and into the natural world opens the mind to wonder and awe.

There's a library of scientific research to show that spending time in natural environments enhances our mental and physical health in life-changing ways – boosting happiness, positivity and wellbeing, and even alleviating depression and anxiety.

Spending time in nature also creates a shift in perception, making space for dreaming and manifestation. Being outside helps us to step away from our day-to-day worries. It's a chance to 'blow away the cobwebs' and focus on the bigger picture, both physically and mentally.

You, too, are a part of all this. You belong to the natural world; you share the same atoms and breathe the same air. Mother Earth created you and sustains you. You are not a separate entity, but a part of the whole fathomless universe. And when you feel this bond, something magical happens: your energy will rise and you will discover a whole new emotional and spiritual connection with Mother Earth.

“Nature is my manifestation of God.”

*Frank Lloyd Wright*

“Nature is the source of all true knowledge.”

*Leonardo da Vinci*

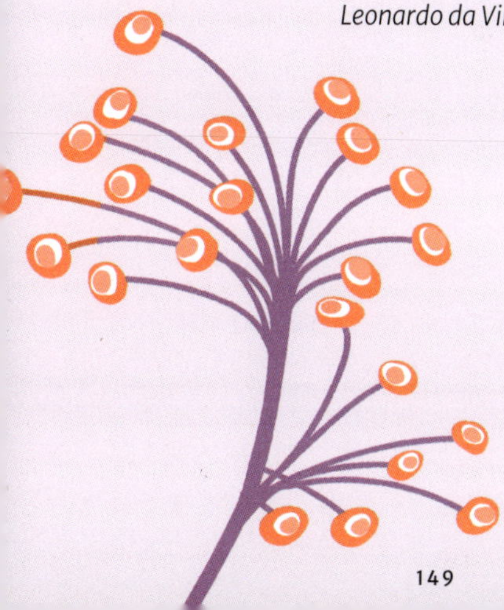

# Manifesting with nature

Given the huge benefits of connecting with the natural world, there is no better way to enhance both your life and your manifesting practice than getting close to nature and being at one with it. Here are some things to try.

- **Practise eco-meditation:** Meditation doesn't have to be seated or practised indoors; walking in nature is a wonderful way to meditate. Engage all your senses by listening to the birds singing and the wind whistling; notice the air on your cheeks, the scent of the earth and the colours that surround you.

- **Get engaged:** Feed the birds, plant trees, sow flowers, grow vegetables ... When you make physical connections with the Earth, spiritual connections grow.

- **Get closer to nature:** Walk barefoot, roll down hills, lie under the stars, hug a tree (yes, really!), swim in open water (as long as it's safe to do so) or even try skinny-dipping.

- **Demonstrate love and respect:** The more you feel at one with Mother Nature, the more you want to protect her. Adopting eco-conscious behaviours, like buying and living sustainably, enhances your own wellbeing and helps protect the planet.

- **Use nature-focused affirmations:** For example:

  I belong to the universe.
  I am a child of nature.

"TO LET LIFE HAPPEN TO YOU IS IRRESPONSIBLE. TO CREATE YOUR DAY IS YOUR DIVINE RIGHT."

Ramtha

"The miracle is not to walk on water. The miracle is to walk on the green earth, dwelling deeply in the present moment and feeling truly alive."

*Thích Nhất Hạnh*

# Harness the power of a new moon

The arrival of the new moon symbolises new beginnings. It's the perfect time to set your intentions and manifest your deepest desires.

The first phase of the moon is when the illuminated side faces away from the Earth; it's the darkest time of the lunar calendar, which creates an opportunity for rest and introspection.

When the next new moon arrives, try this simple meditation.

- Close your eyes and take a few deep breaths.
- Imagine sitting under a clear, night sky, with the moon hidden from view. (You could even do this outside.)
- As darkness surrounds you, welcome a sense of stillness.

- Visualise a seed in the palm of your hand. This tiny seed represents new beginnings.
- Now focus on the areas of your life you would like to transform. Spend some time clarifying your intentions.
- Imagine planting your intentions like seeds in the earth. Visualise roots forming and a shoot pushing through the soil. Watch as leaves unfurl and flowers bloom. These are your dreams unfolding.
- Acknowledge this moment of new beginnings and feel the excitement swell in your heart.
- As you bring your awareness back to the present, quietly thank the universe for its guidance.

"Know in your heart that all things are possible. We couldn't conceive of a miracle if none had ever happened."

*Libbie Fudim*

"Three things cannot be long hidden: the sun, the moon, and the truth."

*Buddha*

# Notice the signs

When you manifest, it's important to look out for evidence that the universe is listening and responding. Signs and synchronicities are clues that things are aligning. Here are some examples of these indications.

- **Repeating patterns:** Do you keep seeing the same number or colour? Does the same word, phrase or song keep cropping up? Repetition can be a strong indication that the universe is working towards bringing your desires into being.

- **People just 'appearing':** Have you heard from someone you've recently been thinking about, bumped into someone in an unexpected place or repeatedly run into the same person? Could there be an energetic connection?

- **Dreams:** When you're asleep, your subconscious is awake to signs from the universe. Take note of recurring themes or dreams that stir powerful emotions; they may be trying to tell you something.

- **Spirit animals:** If an animal crosses your path in unusual circumstances (or even in a dream) it could be your spirit animal delivering a message. Certain animals carry certain symbols, so it's worth looking into …

It can be easy to put unexplained events down to coincidence, but if something resonates with you – if it gives you goosebumps or you just can't get it out of your mind – it's worth paying attention!

"A mind is like a parachute.
It doesn't work if it isn't open."

*Frank Zappa*

"You just can't let life happen to you, you have to make life happen."

*Idowu Koyenikan*

# Keep going

Manifesting takes faith and courage: faith in the power of the universe, and the courage to believe in yourself. But if you find yourself having a wobble along the way, don't worry – that's completely normal. Here are some tips to bear in mind.

- **Keep it real:** Dreaming big can be empowering and exciting – but expecting too much too soon can lead to anxiety and self-doubt. So, while there's no limit to what you can manifest, remember to focus on the process, not just the result. And take a reality check once in a while.

- **Be patient:** Manifesting doesn't happen overnight. Expecting an instant fix only sets you up for disappointment. Remind yourself that good things take time.

- **Check in with someone:** Sharing your dreams with a family member or trusted friend can help them feel more tangible. Other people can also be a source of support when you need a boost.

- **Never mind the roadblocks:** Sometimes life throws us a curveball that throws us off course – a bout of flu, an unexpected or upsetting event, or just a bad day … Don't beat yourself up. Remember that every day is a new opportunity that brings you closer to your dream life.

"You can't go back and make a new start, but you can start right now and make a brand-new ending."

*James R. Sherman*

"JUST BELIEVE IN YOURSELF. EVEN IF YOU DON'T, JUST PRETEND THAT YOU DO AND, AT SOME POINT, YOU WILL."

Venus Williams

# Manifesting love

We all need to be loved, but sometimes it can be hard to know where to start and who to trust. So, if you'd rather manifest than swipe, here are some simple steps to follow.

- **Decide what you're looking for:** Whether it's fun and frolics or marriage and kids, you need to figure out what your ideal relationship looks like.

- **Get excited:** Imagine you have already met 'the one'. Picture yourself in a passionate embrace, sharing a romantic dinner or walking hand in hand. Feel the joy of your manifestation coming true.

- **Write it down:** Putting your intentions into black and white helps solidify them and gives you something to return to.

- **Align your behaviour:** Manifesting isn't magic; it requires action, too. Look out for signs that someone could be a potential partner, trust your instincts and be bold.

- **Let the good vibes flow:** To be a magnet for love you need to radiate love into the world – and this starts with loving yourself. You'll then be ready to receive love in return.

## Affirmations for manifesting love

- I attract love into my life.
- I am beautiful, inside and out.

"Love can only be found through the act of loving."

*Paulo Coelho*

"The secret of manifesting your dreams is believing that you already have them."

*Rhonda Byrne*

# Manifesting prosperity

Who wouldn't like to be richer? Manifesting might not buy you a winning lottery ticket, but it could lead to greater prosperity. Here are some steps you can take.

- **Challenge limiting beliefs:** If you feel guilty about wanting more money, or feel incapable of attracting it, you'll never get rich. The key is to change your negative mindset to a positive one.

- **Imagine you are already wealthy:** This doesn't mean racking up a huge credit card bill; instead, shift your mindset to one of abundance. Like attracts like, so if you focus on a lack of wealth, that is what you will attract. Instead, imagine receiving your desired salary and how it will make you feel.

- **Express gratitude:** Be thankful for the wealth you have already, however little that may be. Remember – you attract more of what you think about.

- **Align your actions:** As the saying goes, 'money doesn't grow on trees'. It's up to you to identify the steps you can take towards prosperity. So, request that pay rise, start that side hustle or draw up a financial plan.

“Whether you think you can, or you think you can’t – you’re right.”

*Henry Ford*

"You don't have to see the whole staircase, just take the first step."

Dr Martin Luther King Jr

# Manifesting your dream job

Work is where many of us spend the majority of our time, so use these steps to manifest a job you truly love.

- **Have clear ambitions:** You can't land your ideal job if you don't know what that is. What does it entail? Where do you want to be in five years' time? Focus on what you want, not what you don't want, and consider using a career or life coach if you need guidance.

- **Release self-doubt:** Identify and replace limiting beliefs with positive ones. Believing in yourself frees up space for opportunities to arise.

- **Visualise it:** Imagine living out your perfect working day. Get creative by writing it down or creating a vision board. Feel the positive emotions associated with realising your ambitions.

- **Align your actions:** Surround yourself with people who support and inspire you. Immerse yourself in seminars, books, training and networking events, and seek opportunities that align with your goals.

- **Have faith:** It might take time, but stay persistent and believe in your manifestation process.

### Affirmations for manifesting your dream career

- I have what it takes to be successful.
- My perfect job is within reach.

"Above all, be the heroine of your life, not the victim."

*Nora Ephron*

"You cannot swim for new horizons until you have courage to lose sight of the shore."

*William Faulkner*

# Manifest the person you want to become

When we think about manifesting, we often think about the things we'd like to attract – more money, a devoted partner, a bigger house, a better job ... There is nothing wrong with any of these; you deserve a life that's filled with abundance and happiness.

However, it's also important to think beyond the material – to consider the feelings, qualities and values that help us to live rich, meaningful and contented lives.

Spend some time thinking about the person you want to become, not just about the things you'd like to have. What are the qualities that really matter to you? Here are a few ideas to get you started. Be sure to add your own values to the list.

Calmer

More adventurous

More loving

Less overwhelmed

More courageous

More sociable and outgoing

More carefree

More creative

More compassionate

Happier

More playful

More skilful or accomplished

More spontaneous

More spiritual

More focused

When you focus on becoming the person you want to be, you will find it easier to manifest your material desires, too.

"Your heart knows the way.
Run in that direction."

*Rumi*

"Your vision will become clear only when you can look into your own heart. Who looks outside, dreams; who looks inside, awakes."

*C.G. Jung*

# Check in with yourself

Now that you are nearing the end of this book, it's a good time to check in with yourself. Spend some time thinking about the following questions.

- Have you manifested anything in your life already; if so, what?
- How did it make you feel?
- What are you manifesting right now?
- What steps have you taken so far on your current manifesting journey?
- Where are you on your road to realising your desires?
- What are the next steps you can take?

This is also a good opportunity to remind yourself of the qualities that will make you grow to be an even more powerful manifester.

- I am open to new experiences.
- I have a positive relationship with myself and others.
- I am kind and grateful.
- I am optimistic.
- My life has meaning and purpose.
- I practise self-care.
- I am spontaneous.
- I see the good around me.
- I am passionate about my life.
- I expect amazing things to happen to me.

Checking in with yourself helps you to stay on track or to change your approach, if necessary. It also allows you to appreciate how far you have come.

"If you have a positive frame of mind, you can manifest positive things in your life."

*Alesha Dixon*

"I'd rather regret the risks that didn't work out than the chances I didn't take at all."

*Simone Biles*

# One last thing

You've set your intentions, you've defined your goals, you've aligned yourself with the law of attraction and trusted in the universe. And voila: the universe has delivered. Congratulations!

Receiving your blessings is a truly wonderful and affirming experience. It's the moment your desires become reality; the moment you can finally say, "I'm living proof that manifesting works."

There's just one more thing to do ... When someone gifts you something special, however large or small, it's only right to say thank you. The same goes for the universe. The final act of manifesting is to express thanks for whatever it is you've received. So, go ahead – write a thank you letter to the universe, shout your gratitude from the rooftops of social media, throw a party if you like!

Gratitude amplifies your positive energy, leading you to attract even more of what you desire and a life that's overflowing with abundance. This means there really is no limit to the amount you can manifest. So, celebrate your progress and express gratitude as often as you can.

“Be grateful more than anything in your life.”

*Taylor Swift*

"Gratitude opens the door to ... the power, the wisdom, the creativity of the universe."

*Elbert Hubbard*

# And finally ...

Congratulations on reaching the end of this book and on discovering the power of manifesting. You already have what it takes to shape your own life and to be everything you've ever wanted. Your dream life is already there, lying in your subconscious, waiting to be set free – to be thought into existence.

Manifesting is simply a tool through which you can harness the power of your thoughts, emotions, intentions and actions to attract the life you desire. This, combined with gratitude and self-belief, is the key to unlocking the door to opportunities you never knew existed. Now it's over to you. So, dream big, enjoy the journey and embrace your best life!

"By thought, the thing you want is brought to you; by action, you receive it."

*Wallace D. Wattles*